OUR
GRE★T
STATES

WHAT'S GREAT ABOUT
ALABAMA?

✳ Jamie Kallio

◯ LERNER PUBLICATIONS COMPANY ✳ MINNEAPOLIS

CONTENTS

ALABAMA WELCOMES YOU! * 4

Content Consultant: Henry McKiven, Associate
Professor of History, University of South
Alabama

Lerner Publications Company
A division of Lerner Publishing Group, Inc.
241 First Avenue North
Minneapolis, MN 55401 USA

For reading levels and more information, look
up this title at www.lernerbooks.com.

Main body text set in ITC Franklin Gothic Std
Book Condensed 12/15.
Typeface provided by Adobe Systems.

Library of Congress Cataloging-in-Publication
Data

Kallio, Jamie.
    What's great about Alabama? / by
Jamie Kallio.
        pages   cm. — (Our great states)
    Includes index.
    ISBN 978-1-4677-3343-4 (lib. bdg. :
alk. paper)
    ISBN 978-1-4677-4704-2 (eBook)
    1. Alabama—Juvenile literature. I. Title.
F326.3.K35 2015
976.1—dc 3   2014008834

Manufactured in the United States of America
1 - PC - 7/15/14

US SPACE & ROCKET CENTER * 6

CATHEDRAL CAVERNS STATE PARK * 8

EARLYWORKS CHILDREN'S MUSEUM * 10

SCI-QUEST HANDS-ON SCIENCE CENTER * 12

BIRMINGHAM ZOO * 14

SPLASH ADVENTURE WATER PARK ✷ 16

CHILDREN'S HANDS-ON MUSEUM ✷ 18

MOUNDVILLE ARCHAEOLOGICAL PARK ✷ 20

BATTLESHIP MEMORIAL PARK ✷ 22

THE ESTUARIUM ✷ 24

ALABAMA BY MAP ✷ 26

ALABAMA FACTS ✷ 28

GLOSSARY ✷ 30

FURTHER INFORMATION ✷ 31

INDEX ✷ 32

Alabama Welcomes You!

Welcome to Alabama! Alabama is known for its hot and humid weather. The warm air lets people enjoy the outdoors year-round. You can camp or hike at Cathedral Caverns State Park. Or go swimming in the ocean and learn about the coast. Alabama has a lot of history. American Indians lived here before anyone else. You can visit American Indian burial grounds in Moundville. Maybe you like outer space. The first rocket launch happened in Huntsville. Visit the US Space & Rocket Center to learn more about the launch. Alabama has many exciting things to see and do. There is something for everyone! Read on to learn about ten places that make Alabama great. You may even want to plan a trip!

Explore Alabama's cities and all the places in between! Just turn the page to find out about the HEART OF DIXIE. >

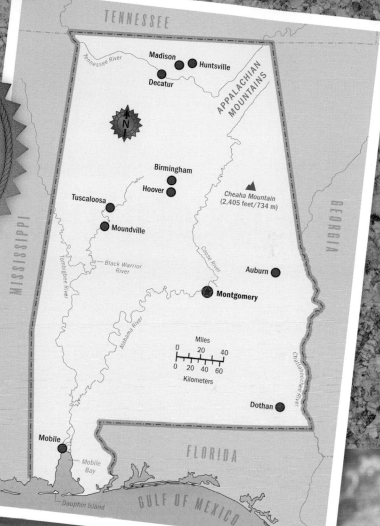

TENNESSEE

Madison
Huntsville
Decatur

APPALACHIAN MOUNTAINS

N

Birmingham
Hoover

Cheaha Mountain
(2,405 feet/734 m)

Tuscaloosa

Moundville

Black Warrior River

Coosa River

Auburn

Montgomery

Miles
0   20   40
0 20 40 60
Kilometers

Dothan

Mobile

Mobile Bay

FLORIDA

Dauphin Island

GULF OF MEXICO

MISSISSIPPI

Tombigbee River

Alabama River

Tennessee River

GEORGIA

Chattahoochee River

US SPACE & ROCKET CENTER

> Huntsville is where the US space program began. The US Space & Rocket Center is one of the largest space museums in the world. Here, you can learn about space program history in Alabama. Start by learning about the space race. The space race was a competition between the United States and the USSR (a former country made up of fifteen republics, including modern-day Russia) to see which nation could make more advances in space science. You'll also see equipment from astronaut training at the museum.

Have you ever wondered what a rocket launch feels like? Take a ride on the Space Shot. This simulator shoots riders 140 feet (43 meters) up in 2.5 seconds! Be sure to stop by the Mars Mission. You can visit and explore Mars in this simulator. Take a rest at the Spacedome IMAX Theater. See a space movie. You'll feel as if you're on the moon or sitting on a space shuttle.

End your day with a bus tour to the Marshall Space Flight Center. This is a working NASA space center. You'll see the Redstone Test Stand and rocket park.

UNITED STATES

See space shuttles up close at the US Space & Rocket Center.

LUNAR ROVER STORAGE

REDSTONE TEST STAND

The Redstone Test Stand is a 75-foot (23 m) frame. It was built in 1953 to test rockets. On May 5, 1961, Alan B. Shepard Jr. was the first American in space. He flew the Mercury-Redstone 3 rocket. The Redstone Test Stand is now a national historic landmark.

CATHEDRAL CAVERNS
STATE PARK

> Cathedral Caverns is a popular location in Marshall County. The caverns have a big entrance. It measures 126 feet (38 m) across and 25 feet (8 m) high!

Inside are 3 acres (1.2 hectares) of stalagmites. Stalagmites are pointed rocks formed from dripping water. Stalagmites grow up from the ground. Explore the cave with a tour guide. You'll see the Mystery River and the Frozen Waterfall rock formation.

Go gem mining after the cave tour. Purchase a bag of dirt and pick through it. Wash the stones in running water. Find out which gems you have using the gemstone display as your reference.

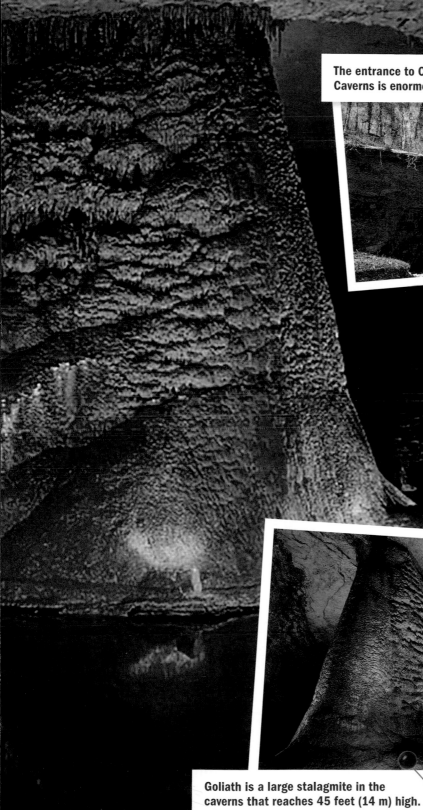

The entrance to Cathedral Caverns is enormous.

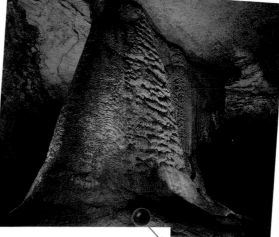

Goliath is a large stalagmite in the caverns that reaches 45 feet (14 m) high.

EARLYWORKS CHILDREN'S MUSEUM

> EarlyWorks Children's Museum in Huntsville is three museums in one! First, visit the Alabama Constitution Village. Dress in colonial outfits and help with chores. Try woodworking, printing, and weaving.

Next, move on to the EarlyWorks Children's History Museum. Get ready to hear an adventure story from the Talking Tree! Build a house at the Kidstruction Zone. Then play some instruments at the Alabama bandstand.

End your day at Huntsville Depot and Museum. There is a robotic ticket agent named Andy. Listen as Andy talks about Alabama's railroad history. Climb aboard a train replica, and explore the inside of a car. Stop in the Auto House room to learn more about cars and trucks. Try on a firefighter costume, and pretend to drive an old fire truck!

Visit the General Store in the history museum where you can pretend to buy and sell food and other goods.

The Huntsville Depot was built in 1860.

THE HISTORIC HUNTSVILLE DEPOT
ALABAMA'S TRANSPORTATION MUSEUM

Ball pythons curl into a ball when scared.

SCI-QUEST HANDS-ON SCIENCE CENTER

> If you like science, then the Sci-Quest Hands-On Science Center is for you! This Huntsville center has more than one hundred exhibits to explore. There's so much to do, you won't know where to start!

Build a roller coaster, catch a falling planet, or play the giant floor piano. Check out the Wave Tank. View yourself in the Fun House mirrors. Then shout into the Echo Tube. And who can pass up the Barf Machine?

The Science Center also has many pets. Get up close with a Russian tortoise and a ball python. Norma the crested gecko has no tail. Be sure to say hello to her at the front desk!

End your day relaxing in the theater. It shows cool 3-D science movies. Touch-screen monitors let you pick your own adventure!

Burps and Belches

Cultural Factoid
In some countries burping is considered a compliment to the cook.

Everyone burps. Burping, belching and eructation (eh ruct TA shun) are all names for the same thing.

Burps form in your stomach. Your stomach is connected on one end to your esophagus, which reaches up to your throat. The other end connects to your intestines. There is always a little bit of gas in the upper half of your stomach.

When you eat and drink, you swallow air, which adds more gas to the foods

Factoid
People who eat fast, talk while they chew, or smoke burp more often. Why? It's because they're swallowing lots of air.

Factoid
Some people burp more than other people. Their burps might not get up their foods or their lower esophageal sphincter might open at a stomach pressure.

BURP-O-METER

Soda

Try standing straight after spinning fast on the Angular Momentum machine.

BIRMINGHAM ZOO

> Stop for a visit at the Birmingham Zoo. Eight hundred different animals live here! The zoo has a special exhibit called Trails of Africa. It is dedicated to the conservation of African elephants. You will see zebras, rhinos, and giraffes. You can even feed the giraffes!

The zoo also has an area just for kids. It has a petting zoo and a playground. Play in the splash pad on hot days. Dry off with a ride on the carousel. Or jump on the mini train that tours the zoo.

Check out the sea lion training show. And don't forget to feed the lorikeets! Lorikeets are bright birds that flock to you if you're holding nectar. Have you been this close to a bird before?

Sign up for an exciting Twilight Tour. The zoo looks different in the dark! You'll get to see what the animals do at night.

Western lowland gorillas (*left*) and macaws (*right*) are just a few of the animals you may see while walking through the Birmingham Zoo.

SPLASH ADVENTURE WATER PARK

> Splash Adventure Water Park in Bessemer is full of fun things to do. You might have to come back more than once!

Go down one of the park's many waterslides. The Acapulco Drop is a nine-story slide that drops you straight down into a pool. Try the Splashdown. This tube drops you 50 feet (15 m). Then it spins you into the pool below. If you're really brave, try the Upsurge. This 216-foot (66 m) slide has twists and turns.

Catch the waves at the wave pool. If you need to dry off, check out the zip line. When you're ready to relax, hang out on the Black Warrior River.

Take a ride down a water slide *(left)* or speed down a zip line *(right)* at Splash Adventure!

Cool off in the Mist-ical Maze with friends.

17

CHILDREN'S HANDS-ON MUSEUM

> When you're in Tuscaloosa, stop at the Children's Hands-On Museum. The museum has three floors and twenty-three exhibits to explore. You can try on old-fashioned clothes. Step back in time in the Choctaw Indian Village. Make pottery or a shell necklace.

Have you ever wondered what the inside of a beaver dam looks like? Find out when you climb through Beaver's Bend. Use giant microscopes to look at lizards, crabs, and turtles. Maybe you would like to be a farmer when you grow up. Head over to Lil' Sprouts Farmer's Market. Load your crops into your truck, and go to the market!

Visit the health system room. You can be a nurse, a doctor, or a patient. End your day on a towboat. You'll learn more about the Black Warrior River.

Measure your height in the doctor's office exhibit.

RIVER TRANSPORTATION

There are many rivers in Alabama. People started using steamboats to travel in the early 1800s. People also transported goods by using steamboats. Towns grew along the rivers. Alabama's economy would not have grown as quickly without steamboats.

MOUNDVILLE
ARCHAEOLOGICAL PARK

> American Indians known as Mound Builders lived in Alabama more than one thousand years ago. They have this name because they built huge earth mounds. Moundville was a large American Indian settlement along the Black Warrior River.

Visit Moundville Archaeological Park. You will see twenty-six mounds. The tallest mound is 58 feet (18 m) high! Make sure to stop at the Jones Archaeological Museum. Inside are more than two hundred American Indian objects. These include clothing, pottery, and artwork. You can even explore an earth lodge.

The park celebrates the Moundville Native American Festival in October. Watch experts shoot arrows or throw spears and darts. Try a game of stickball or throw an American Indian football. Dress like an American Indian and make a shell necklace. Listen to stories, see dancing, and hear music.

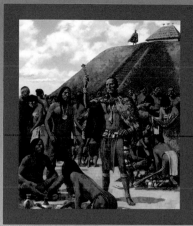

MOUND BUILDERS

Why did some American Indians build mounds? One reason was to bury their dead. Some mounds had temples at the very top. The American Indians built their cities around the mounds. The mounds were made of dirt and clay. They also had shells and volcanic glass in them.

There are many ancient pieces of pottery to see in the Jones Archaeological Museum in Moundville.

BATTLESHIP MEMORIAL PARK

> Battleship Memorial Park is a military history park and museum in Mobile. You can walk twelve decks on the USS *Alabama*. It is a famous warship from World War II (1939–1945).

You will have a chance to be in charge of the ship's guns. See what it feels like to get locked up in the ship's jail, called the brig. Try out the bunks where the crew slept. Go below water in the submarine USS *Drum*. The *Drum* is the oldest US submarine on display in the world! It was launched on May 12, 1941.

Walk and explore the ship's deck. Visit the Aircraft Pavilion. It is filled with more than twenty-five old aircraft from four wars.

Visitors can climb into the Flight Simulator. This machine makes it look and feel as if you are flying! Take the controls and choose which mission you want to fly. Don't miss this airborne trip!

Explore the many decks on the USS *Alabama* during your visit.

LUCKY A

The USS *Alabama* was nicknamed Lucky A by her crew because she never lost a fight. In World War II, the battleship was involved in every major fight in the Pacific Ocean and never took damage. The ship earned nine battle stars, which are badges of honor for completing missions in war.

THE ESTUARIUM

> The Dauphin Island Sea Lab in Dauphin Island is Alabama's main marine center. Education and research happen here. Part of the sea lab is called the Estuarium. This is a public aquarium with animals from Mobile Bay.

Walk through the Living Marsh Boardwalk. You'll see crabs, lobsters, eels, and sharks. See if you can spot native birds flying overhead. Climb aboard the *Miss MayMay*. This interactive boat has many activities. Climb through a shrimp net or help guide the boat.

The Gulf of Mexico tank holds 16,000 gallons (60,570 liters) of water. You'll see sand sharks, colorful fish, and coral. Stop by the touch tanks and pet a stingray. Explore a replica of an old French sailing ship. You will find many underwater treasures on board!

Take a walk through a salt marsh, and learn more about the animals that live in this habitat.

ALABAMA BY MAP

> MAP KEY

⭐ Capital city

⬤ City

◉ Point of interest

▲ Highest elevation

—·· — State border

Visit www.lerneresource.com to learn more about the state flag of Alabama.

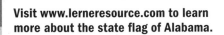

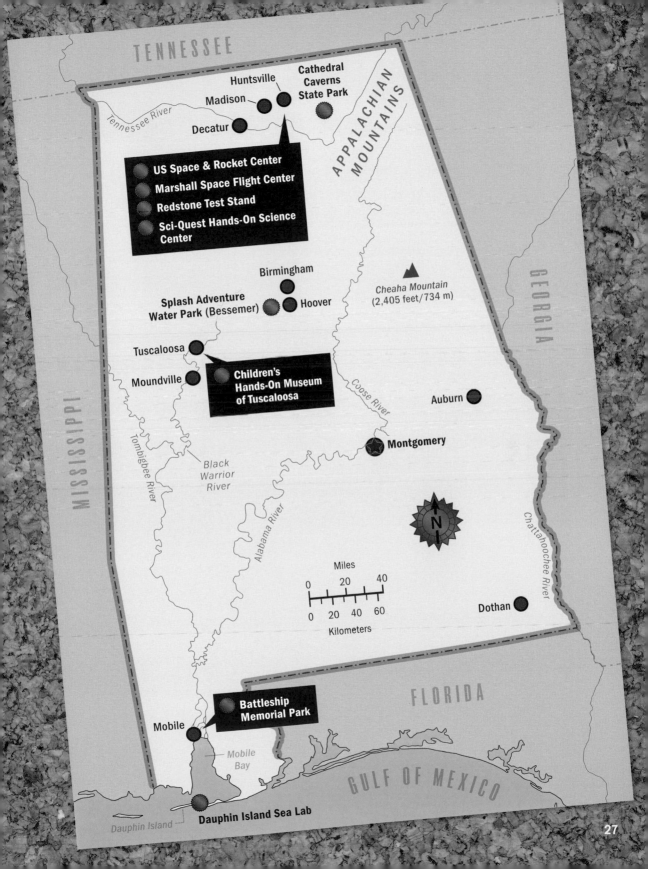

TENNESSEE

Tennessee River

Huntsville
Madison
Decatur

Cathedral
Caverns
State Park

APPALACHIAN MOUNTAINS

US Space & Rocket Center
Marshall Space Flight Center
Redstone Test Stand
Sci-Quest Hands-On Science Center

GEORGIA

Birmingham

Splash Adventure
Water Park (Bessemer)

Hoover

Cheaha Mountain
(2,405 feet/734 m)

Tuscaloosa

Moundville

Children's
Hands-On Museum
of Tuscaloosa

Coose River

Auburn

MISSISSIPPI

Tombigbee River

Black
Warrior
River

Montgomery

Alabama River

N

Chattahoochee River

Miles
0   20   40
0   20 40 60
Kilometers

Dothan

Battleship
Memorial Park

Mobile

Mobile
Bay

FLORIDA

GULF OF MEXICO

Dauphin Island

Dauphin Island Sea Lab

ALABAMA FACTS

NICKNAME: the Heart of Dixie

SONG: "Alabama," written by Julia S. Tutwiler; composed by Edna Gockel Gussen

MOTTO: *Audemus jura nostra defendere*, or "We Dare Defend Our Rights"

> **FLOWER:** camellia

TREE: southern longleaf pine

BIRD: yellowhammer woodpecker

> **ANIMAL:** black bear

FOODS: pecans, peaches, blackberries

DATE AND RANK OF STATEHOOD: December 14, 1819; the 22nd state

> **CAPITAL:** Montgomery

AREA: 51,701 square miles (134,403 sq. km)

AVERAGE JANUARY TEMPERATURE: 46°F (8°C)

AVERAGE JULY TEMPERATURE: 80°F (27°C)

POPULATION AND RANK: 4,822,023; 23rd (2012)

MAJOR CITIES AND POPULATIONS: Birmingham (212,237), Montgomery (205,764), Mobile (195,111), Huntsville (180,105), Tuscaloosa (90,468)

NUMBER OF US CONGRESS MEMBERS: *7* representatives, 2 senators

NUMBER OF ELECTORAL VOTES: 9

NATURAL RESOURCES: coal, oil

> **AGRICULTURAL PRODUCTS:** cattle, chicken, eggs, cotton

MANUFACTURED GOODS: chemicals, food products, paper products, metal products, transportation equipment

STATE HOLIDAYS AND CELEBRATIONS: Alabama Renaissance Faire, Dothan's National Peanut Festival

brig: a jail or prison of the US Navy

conservation: the protection of animals, plants, and natural resources

earth lodge: a building made from earth or sod, often supported on a wooden frame, and often placed partially below the surface of the ground

economy: the process or system by which goods and services are produced, sold, and bought in a country or region

launch: to send or shoot something, such as a rocket, into the air, water, or outer space

marine: of or relating to the sea or the plants and animals that live in the sea

nectar: a sweet liquid produced by plants

replica: an exact or very close copy of something

shuttle: a spacecraft that can be used more than once and that carries people into outer space and back to Earth

simulator: a machine that is used to show what something looks or feels like and is usually used to study something or to train people

LERNER

SOURCE™

Expand learning beyond the printed book. Download free, complementary educational resources for this book from our website, www.lerneresource.com.

FURTHER INFORMATION

Brown, Dottie. *Alabama*. Minneapolis: Lerner Publications, 2002. This book talks about Alabama's role during the Civil War (1861–1865). It also discusses Alabama's weather, such as tornadoes and hurricanes.

Enchanted Learning
http://www.enchantedlearning.com/usa/states/alabama
If you're looking for crafts and activities about Alabama, this is the website to visit!

Heos, Bridget. *Alabama: Past and Present*. New York: Rosen, 2010. Learn more about Alabama's place in history, especially its role in government and industry.

The Official Travel Site of Alabama
http://alabama.travel
This website is packed with travel information about Alabama. Check out the section about family-fun road trips across the state!

The Official Website of the State of Alabama
http://www.alabama.gov/portal/secondary.jsp?id=~kidsPage
Located on Alabama's official website is a special section just for kids!

Tieck, Sarah. *Alabama*. Minneapolis: Abdo Publishing, 2013. Get in-depth information about famous people in Alabama, the popular cities, and a look at sports.

INDEX

Battleship Memorial Park, 22

Bessemer, 16

Birmingham Zoo, 14

Black Warrior River, 16, 18, 20

Cathedral Caverns State Park, 4, 8

Children's Hands-On Museum, 18

Dauphin Island, 24

Dauphin Island Sea Lab, 24

EarlyWorks Children's Museum, 10

Estuarium, 24

Huntsville, 4, 6, 10

Jones Archaeological Museum, 20

maps, 5, 26–27

Marshall County, 8

Marshall Space Flight Center, 6

Mobile, 22

Mound Builders, 20–21

Moundville, 4, 20

Moundville Archaeological Park, 20

NASA, 6

Redstone Test Stand, 6–7

Sci-Quest Hands-On Science Center, 12

Shepard, Alan B., Jr., 7

Splash Adventure Water Park, 16

Tuscaloosa, 18

USS Alabama, 22–23

USS Drum, 22

US Space & Rocket Center, 4, 6

PHOTO ACKNOWLEDGMENTS

The images in this book are used with the permission of: © Jason Patrick Ross/Shutterstock Images, p. 1; © Sean Pavone Photo/iStockphoto, p. 4; © iStockphoto/Thinkstock, pp. 5 (bottom), 12, 17 (left), 17 (right), 19, 29 (top), 29 (middle top), 29 (bottom); © Laura Westlund/Independent Picture Service, pp. 5 (top), 27; Library of Congress, pp. 6–7 (LC-DIG-highsm-07824), 7 (top) (LC-DIG-highsm-07833), 7 (bottom) (LC-DIG-highsm-09004), 8–9 (LC-DIG-highsm-06877), 9 (bottom) (LC-DIG-highsm-06879), 10–11 (LC-DIG-highsm-07774), 11 (top) (LC-DIG-highsm-07789), 12–13 (LC-DIG-highsm-07809), 20–21 (LC-DIG-highsm-05878), 23 (bottom) (LC-DIG-highsm-05161), © Jeff Greenberg /Alamy, pp. 9 (top), 13, 14–15, 18, 18–19, 24–25; © Andre Jenny Stock Connection Worldwide/Newscom, p. 11 (bottom); © Dane Jorgensen /Shutterstock Images, p. 15 (left); Ralph Daily, p. 15 (right); © Michelle Campbell/The Birmingham News/AP Images, pp. 16–17; © H. Tom Hall /National Geographic Image Collection /Glow Images, p. 21 (top); C.B. Moore /Public Domain, p. 21 (bottom); © Glow Images, pp. 22–23; © Stockbyte /Thinkstock, p. 23 (top); © Stephen Saks Photography/Alamy, p. 25; © nicoolay/iStockphoto, p. 26; © Perry Watson/Thinkstock, p. 29 (middle bottom).

Cover: © Tad Denson-MyShotz.com, and The Alabama Tourism Department (USS Alabama); The Alabama Department of Tourism/Huntsville Convention & Visitors Bureau (Cathedral Caverns); The Alabama Department of Tourism (Splash Water Park); © Laura Westlund/Independent Picture Service (map); © iStockphoto. com/fpm (seal); © iStockphoto.com/ vicm (pushpins); © iStockphoto.com/ benz190 (corkboard).